TABLE OF CONTENTS

Synopsis 1

Background Information 2

Pre-Reading Activities .... 3 - 4

June 14 - December 22, 1942 .... 5 - 7

January 13 - July 26, 1943 .... 8 - 10

July 29 - December 29, 1943 .... 11 - 12

January 2 - March 12, 1944 .... 13 - 14

March 14 - May 2, 1944 .... 15 - 16

May 3 - August 1, 1944 .... 17 - 18

Cloze Activity 19

Post-Reading Activities 20

Suggestions For Further Reading 21

Answer Key .... 22 - 23

Notes 24

Novel-Ties® are printed on recycled paper.

The purchase of this study guide entitles an individual teacher to reproduce pages for use in a classroom. Reproduction for use in an entire school or school system or for commercial use is prohibited. Beyond the classroom use by an individual teacher, reproduction, transmittal or retrieval of this work is prohibited without written permission from the publisher.

Copyright © 1987, 2004, 2012 by LEARNING LINKS

For the Teacher

This reproducible study guide to use in conjunction with *Anne Frank: The Diary of a Young Girl* consists of lessons for guided reading. Written in chapter-by-chapter format, the guide contains a synopsis, pre-reading activities, vocabulary and comprehension exercises, as well as extension activities to be used as follow-up to the novel.

In a homogeneous classroom, whole class instruction with one title is appropriate. In a heterogeneous classroom, reading groups should be formed: each group works on a different novel at its reading level. Depending upon the length of time devoted to reading in the classroom, each novel, with its guide and accompanying lessons, may be completed in three to six weeks.

Begin using NOVEL-TIES for reading development by distributing the novel and a folder to each child. Distribute duplicated pages of the study guide for students to place in their folders. After examining the cover and glancing through the book, students can participate in several pre-reading activities. Vocabulary questions should be considered prior to reading a chapter; all other work should be done after the chapter has been read. Comprehension questions can be answered orally or in writing. The classroom teacher should determine the amount of work to be assigned, always keeping in mind that readers must be nurtured and that the ultimate goal is encouraging students' love of reading.

The benefits of using NOVEL-TIES are numerous. Students read good literature in the original, rather than in abridged or edited form. The good reading habits, formed by practice in focusing on interpretive comprehension and literary techniques, will be transferred to the books students read independently. Passive readers become active, avid readers.

ANNE FRANK: THE DIARY OF A YOUNG GIRL

SYNOPSIS

When Anne Frank turned thirteen, she received a gift that allowed her to share her feelings and dreams with a completely sympathetic "friend"—a diary that she named "Kitty." This diary became Anne's constant companion to whom she communicated her private thoughts and observations. These observations coupled universal adolescent longings with a poignant expression of the unique tragedy of the times in which she lived, for Anne was a Jewish child growing up in Holland during World War II.

Because of Adolph Hitler's determination to exterminate the Jewish people, Anne and her family fled Germany only to find themselves under Hitler's grasp in Holland. Hitler's war against the Jews affected Anne's family with increasing harshness. Anne and her sister Margot were forced to attend special Jewish schools; their father lost his job; the family could not visit theaters and restaurants. These were minor inconveniences compared to what would await the Franks if captured by the Nazis and placed in concentration camps.

In order to avoid this ultimate disaster, the Frank and Van Daan families went into hiding with the help of Dutch Christian friends. Their home became a few secret rooms above the warehouse Mr. Frank managed; and eight people became a family in the "Secret Annexe," with all of the quarreling, laughing, and sharing such a relationship in close quarters entails.

Throughout her stay in the warehouse, Anne experienced the typical rites of passage of adolescence—even teenage love in the person of Peter Van Daan. Their quiet talks and their first kiss are described in the diary, placed against the background of wartime Holland. Juxtaposing the ordinary routines of everyday existence with the extraordinary demands made by their living conditions, Anne created a vivid picture of all the Secret Annexe inhabitants and the events surrounding them.

Tragically, this account was ended abruptly. Secret police discovered the hideout just months before Holland was liberated from the Nazis. Anne did not survive the horrors of the concentration camp, but her words have lived on as testimony to her unique strength as a person and her talent as a writer. Those who read her words today can only marvel that these perceptive observations were penned by a young girl who was just beginning to experience life.

BACKGROUND INFORMATION

The Holocaust refers to the systematic destruction by Hitler and his National Socialist Party of all those who did not conform to the German ideal of culture and race. Such "undesirables" included people who suffered from mental illness, communists, gypsies, Slavs, homosexuals, and others. Above all, this destruction was aimed at the Jewish people who lived in Germany and in German-occupied countries. This vision of a Pan-Germanic empire where Aryan culture could reign supreme had been espoused by philosophers and writers for more than a hundred years before Hitler's rise to power. It was linked to anti-Semitic sentiment that had smoldered among European nations, especially when economic conditions were poor. Under Hitler, this anti-Semitism received moral, legal, and administrative sanction.

In 1933 conditions were ripe for the downfall of the Weimar Republic and the appointment of Adolph Hitler as chancellor by President Paul Von Hindenburg. Because of a poor economy and the feeling that the Versailles Treaty, which ended World War I, had been an affront to Germany, malcontents like Hitler could flourish. Once in power, Hitler unleashed a reign of terror against those he considered undesirable. At first, government decrees eliminated Jewish participation in German social and cultural life. Soon, Jews were totally isolated from the rest of society. The Nuremburg Laws of 1935 prohibited marriage between Jew and German; Jews were no longer to be considered citizens. They eventually were forced to live in ghettos where disease, hunger, and death were rampant.

Finally, work camps and then death camps were established as the "final solution to the Jewish problem." This final solution was carried out in all of the European countries that Germany occupied during World War II—Poland, France, Holland, Belgium, and Russia.

By 1945, six million Jews, along with many gypsies and Slavic leaders had perished. Jewish-European culture, as it had previously existed, ceased to be. While a handful of European Jews remained to salvage their lives after Hitler's defeat, most had either fled to a more secure place or died from the war Hitler had waged against them.

ANNE FRANK: THE DIARY OF A YOUNG GIRL

PRE-READING ACTIVITIES

1. Read the Background Information on page two of this study guide and do some additional research on the Holocaust. Learn how German anti-Semitism contributed to the rise of Hitler and the Nazi Party, eventually spreading its policies of Jewish extermination to other European nations. Also, learn how Hitler's policies affected Jews and non-Jews in Holland.

2. Create a time-line of major events which occurred in the world during World War II (1939–1945). As you read Anne's diary, refer to the time-line to see what is taking place in the world while Anne and her family are in hiding.

3. Consider how political events often shape the lives of ordinary citizens. What places in the world today have civilian populations suffering due to their government's policies? Has there been any political event or government action that has affected your own life or the lives of others you know?

4. Do some research on conditions of life in Germany as the Nazi party gained power. Try to understand why some Jewish people decided to remain in their homeland and go into hiding rather than try to emigrate. Imagine that you and your family were faced with a hostile government and had to weigh the challenges of leaving your homeland against the dangers of remaining. What do you think you would choose to do?

5. Some people in Nazi-controlled countries, particularly Holland, showed great courage by offering shelter and thus risking their own lives to save people persecuted by Hitler. Contrast them to those in the population who ignored the evidence of large-scale persecution. Faced with a similar dilemma, do you think you would come to the aid of others at the risk of your own life?

6. Keep a reading journal as you complete each segment of the book. In your journal, record your own reactions to what you have read and your feelings about the characters. The journal should also include any predictions or conclusions you may draw about the events described.

7. Before you read the actual diary pages that comprise this book, read the introductory pages which include information on its first publication in 1947 and the Introduction itself, written by Eleanor Roosevelt. This will establish the context in which this extraordinary book was written.

Pre-Reading Activities (cont.)

8. In the Anticipation Guide below are eight statements dealing with the world Anne knew as a teenager growing up in Holland during World War II facing the onslaught of German tyranny. Before you read Anne's diary, tell whether you agree or disagree by writing YES or NO next to each statement under the YOU column. After you finish reading her diary, tell whether Anne would agree with each of the statements by writing YES or NO in the ANNE column.

ANTICIPATION GUIDE

STATEMENT	YOU	ANNE
1. Family members pull together in the face of crisis.		
2. Strangers are always afraid to help those in need.		
3. Facing tragedy makes you mature more rapidly.		
4. People find it easy to change their habits when they need to survive.		
5. Teenage daughters often find it difficult to get along with their mothers.		
6. When survival is the primary concern, romantic love cannot evolve.		
7. When you live with many people, you never feel alone.		
8. Friendship means sharing your thoughts with another person.		

JUNE 14, 1942 – DECEMBER 22, 1942

Vocabulary: Draw a line from each word on the left to its correct definition on the right. Then use the numbered words to fill in the blanks in the sentences below.

1. melancholy
2. devour
3. fanatic
4. superfluous
5. somber
6. trivial
7. obstinate
8. optimism

a. person with extreme zeal or enthusiasm
b. stubborn
c. more than is required; excessive
d. gloomy state of mind
e. of very little importance; insignificant
f. eat hungrily
g. dismal or dull as in color
h. tendency to look on the favorable side of events

· ·

1. Wearing stylish clothing seemed like a(n) _____ matter when war was raging all around us.

2. After being starved at the hands of an unkind master, we watched the dog _____ its food.

3. In many cultures people dress in _____ colors to attend a funeral.

4. He became such a religious _____ that he spent most of his waking hours in prayer, neglecting his work and family.

5. A mood of _____ spread over the entire family when they realized that this was their last reunion until after the war.

6. Despite our pleas, the _____ child refused to heed our warnings about crossing the busy intersection carefully.

7. Sugar is _____ in the already-sweetened iced tea.

8. The girl's _____ was contagious, making us all laugh and joke even while enemy guns were heard in the distance.

ANNE FRANK: THE DIARY OF A YOUNG GIRL

June 14, 1942 – December 22, 1942 (cont.)

Questions:

1. Why did Anne decide to keep a diary? Why did she call the diary "Kitty"?

2. How did the German occupation of Holland affect Anne and her family?

3. What did Anne mean when she wrote on July 8, 1942, "Years seem to have passed between Sunday and now. So much has happened, it is just as if the whole world had turned upside-down"?

4. Who helped the Frank family go into hiding?

5. Where did the Franks and the Van Daans decide to hide?

6. What attempts did Anne and her family make to keep their life as normal as possible?

7. What news from the outside world made Anne realize the desperate conditions that Jews faced?

8. Why wouldn't Anne allow news of the outside world to depress her?

Questions for Discussion:

1. What did the first few pages of the book reveal about the quality of Anne's family life? How concerned did she then seem about the war in Europe?

2. Why do you think people like Miep and Mr. Koophuis wanted to help the Franks and other Jews?

3. Why do you think it was difficult for the eight people to avoid quarreling as they settled into the "Secret Annexe"? Do you think this was a normal reaction, or that they were incompatible families?

4. Compare the feelings Anne had for her mother with those she had for her father. Do you think that these feelings were typical or unusual for a thirteen-year-old girl?

5. Based on the quality of Anne's writing and what she revealed about herself, how would you assess her level of maturity?

Social Studies Connection:

Anne mentioned going to meetings of the Zionist Movement. Do some research into the Zionist Movement. When was it begun? What was its goal? Why was it always a controversial movement even among Jews?

LEARNING LINKS

ANNE FRANK: THE DIARY OF A YOUNG GIRL

June 14, 1942 – December 22, 1942 (cont.)

Activity: Survival in the Annexe

Anne's family prepared for hiding by sending cartons of their possessions to the Annexe. Make a list of the items that you think they would find most useful, keeping in mind the need to conserve space. Only include objects that could have been obtained in 1942. Tell how each item would be used. An example is given to get you started.

Item	Use
radio	to receive news of the outside world

Writing Activity:

Imagine that you are about to leave your home to go into hiding for an indeterminate length of time. Write a journal entry describing this imagined event and your feelings at that time.

JANUARY 13, 1943 – JULY 26, 1943

Vocabulary: Synonyms are words with similar meanings. Draw a line from each word in column A to its synonym in column B. Then use the words in column A to fill in the blanks in the sentences below.

A	B
1. clandestine	a. stopped
2. morale	b. pushy
3. cunning	c. spirit
4. indignant	d. angry
5. ceased	e. criticisms
6. rebukes	f. secret
7. aggressive	g. miserable
8. wretched	h. cleverness

. . . .

1. The family members had to use all of their _____ in order to bring food to the hideout without being discovered.

2. The Nazis had become increasingly _____ in their house-to-house searches, causing many families to go into hiding.

3. All of our activity _____ when the German soldiers made a search of the neighborhood.

4. We would have been taken to prison instantly if the German soldiers became aware of our _____ living quarters.

5. Anne resented the _____ she received from her family and the Van Daans for behavior that was once considered acceptable.

6. Despite their hardships, their love for one another and hope for a better future kept up their _____.

7. Anne appreciated her own life more when she compared it to the _____ conditions of other Jews who had not gone into hiding.

8. Many Jewish families in Holland were _____ about losing their rights and privileges, but grateful to be protected by fellow countrymen.

January 13, 1943 – July 26, 1943 (cont.)

Questions:

1. Why did Anne feel fortunate to live in the "Secret Annexe"?

2. What were the general living conditions in Holland during the war?

3. How did Anne justify her cold attitude toward her mother? Do you think her feelings were justified?

4. On her birthday, Anne called herself "the Benjamin of the family." Since Benjamin was the youngest and favorite brother and son of the biblical Jacob's family, why would such a comparison be fitting on Anne's birthday?

5. Why did Anne's parents consider sending her outdoors with Miep? Why did they decide against the plan?

6. What problem arose between Dussel and Anne because they shared a room? Do you think a conflict between the two was inevitable?

7. Why were the air raids in Holland both frightening and welcome for the Annexe residents?

Questions for Discussion:

1. Do you think that Anne was the only one in the Secret Annexe who was miserable about the confinement?

2. Why do you think small matters took on major significance in the Secret Annexe?

3. Why were books of special significance to the people living in the Annexe?

4. What might happen to Anne and her family if they left the Secret Annexe?

5. From what Anne revealed in her diary, do you think the Dutch people were helpful enough to their Jewish population?

6. Do you think Anne should have behaved better and been more cooperative while she lived in the Annexe?

Social Studies Connection:

When they learned that Mussolini had resigned as leader of Italy, the Secret Annexe residents were overjoyed. Do some research to find out why this event made them believe that the war might end soon.

January 13, 1943 – July 26, 1943 (cont.)

Literary Device: Simile

A simile is a figure of speech in which two unlike objects are compared, using the words "like" or "as." For example:

> . . . mocking looks and accusations which are leveled at me every day, and find their mark, like shafts from a tightly strung bow, and which are just as hard to draw from my body.

What is being compared?

What does this reveal about Anne's feelings?

Writing Activity:

Imagine that you are Anne's friend and are able to write a letter to her. Tell her what you think she needs to hear in order to make her time in the Secret Annexe more bearable.

JULY 29, 1943 – DECEMBER 29, 1943

Vocabulary: Antonyms are words with opposite meanings. Draw a line from each word in column A to its antonym in column B. Then use the words in column A to fill in the blanks in the sentences below.

A	B
1. pedantic	a. indifferent
2. capitulate	b. meager
3. inquisitive	c. tranquility
4. exaggerate	d. concise
5. tolerant	e. resist
6. tumult	f. disapproving
7. hearty	g. understate

. . . .

1. From inside the Annexe they heard the _____ in the streets as bombs dropped and sirens wailed.

2. Anne resented having to share a room with the _____ Mr. Dussel, whose endless advice made her life unbearable.

3. Once Italy had surrendered, the families in the Annexe thought Hitler would soon _____.

4. With the radio as her only communication, Anne became increasingly _____ about the news of the outside world.

5. Living in such close quarters made each person _____ the faults of the others.

6. Everyone dreamed of the _____ meals of the past after existing on meager food rations during the war years.

7. Strong-willed and opinionated, Anne found it difficult to be _____ of anyone else's shortcomings.

ANNE FRANK: THE DIARY OF A YOUNG GIRL

July 29, 1943 – December 29, 1943 (cont.)

Questions:

1. What was extraordinary about what Anne described as an "ordinary day in the Annexe"?

2. Why did the residents of the Annexe become more active after 5:30 in the evening?

3. What evidence showed that Anne was suffering from depression?

4. Why did Elli now have more of the responsibility for helping the people in the Annexe survive?

5. When Anne thought about her friend Lies, what did she imagine?

6. What did Anne believe was the only way to cure loneliness?

Questions for Discussion:

1. Do you think it is natural for the residents of the Annexe to squabble to such a great degree? How do you think you would react to living in such close quarters?

2. How had life changed for the residents of the Annexe from St. Nicholas' Day 1942 to St. Nicholas' Day 1943?

Social Studies Connection:

Do some research in the library or go online to find a facsimile of a newspaper published on September 8, 1943. Compare the newspaper reports of Italy's surrender to the way Anne reported it in her diary.

Writing Activity:

Imagine you are Margot or Peter and write about one of the days Anne described in her diary. Tell about that day from another point of view and comment upon Anne's mood and behavior.

ANNE FRANK: THE DIARY OF A YOUNG GIRL

JANUARY 2, 1944 – MARCH 12, 1944

Vocabulary: Many words in our language can be used in different ways. Knowing how a word is used in one way often helps determine what it means in a different context. Answer the following questions, using a dictionary only if necessary.

1. If something that is <u>complex</u> is made of many different parts describe a <u>building complex</u>.

2. If a <u>maniac</u> behaves in a wild, unpredictable way, how do you feel if you have a <u>mania</u> for something?

3. If the <u>dawn</u> is the beginning of the day when light first appears, what happens when something <u>dawns</u> upon you?

4. If a <u>scrap</u> of paper is something you might throw away, what do you do when you <u>scrap</u> a project?

5. If an <u>embryo</u> is an animal in its first phase of development, what part of a project might be called its <u>embryonic</u> stage?

LEARNING LINKS

January 2, 1944 – March 12, 1944 (cont.)

Questions:

1. Why did Anne originally seek out Peter Van Daan? Why do you think their relationship grew?

2. How did the people in the Annexe get news of the outside world? What topics interested them most?

3. What would happen to Dutch citizens if they were caught helping Jews?

4. What preparations for the English invasion did the people in the Secret Annexe make?

5. How did Anne feel she had changed while living in the Annexe?

6. How did Anne and her mother each think she could relieve depression? Why do you think they had different solutions to the problem of depression?

Questions for Discussion:

1. Do you think Anne judged her mother fairly? Might her feelings have been the same if she were leading a normal life?

2. Do you think Anne's dreams were typical of a teenage girl?

3. Why might Anne turn her thoughts to all the boys who were her boyfriends at this time in her life?

4. Do you think Anne and Peter would have had a romantic relationship in normal times?

Writing Activity:

People have different ways of coping with sadness. What do you do when you are feeling sad or depressed? Do you agree more with Anne's approach or with her mother's? Write about a time when you felt sad. Tell how you coped with your feelings.

ANNE FRANK: THE DIARY OF A YOUNG GIRL

MARCH 14, 1944 – MAY 2, 1944

Vocabulary: Use the context to determine the meaning of the underlined word in each of the following sentences.

1. Because he was such an <u>adroit</u> story-teller, everyone believed him.

   Your definition_____

   Dictionary definition _____

2. A <u>hospitable</u> host never lets his guests go hungry.

   Your definition_____

   Dictionary definition _____

3. Since I don't know what really happened, I will have to <u>speculate</u> that what I heard is true.

   Your definition_____

   Dictionary definition _____

4. Instead of peace and harmony, there was only <u>discord</u>.

   Your definition_____

   Dictionary definition _____

5. Every time we made plans, he seemed to <u>sabotage</u> them so that nothing turned out the way we wanted.

   Your definition_____

   Dictionary definition _____

6. Although she was lonely, her <u>consolation</u> was that he missed her, too.

   Your definition_____

   Dictionary definition _____

Questions:

1. What did Anne mean when she referred to the war that "reigns incessantly within"?
2. Why was "Kitty" becoming an even more valuable companion for Anne?
3. How did Anne help Peter cope with life in the Annexe?
4. How did the war affect life for an ordinary Dutch citizen?

LEARNING LINKS

March 14, 1944 – May 2, 1944 (cont.)

5. What were Anne's dreams for the future? Based upon what you know of Anne from her diary, do you think she might have realized these dreams?

6. Why did the residents of the Secret Annexe feel threatened by a burglary at the warehouse?

7. Why was April 15, 1944 an important day for Anne?

8. How did Anne's father feel about the relationship between Anne and Peter? Do you think his feelings were justified?

Questions for Discussion:

1. Why do you think it was important for Anne to communicate her feelings about Peter to her sister Margot? Do you think Margot was as gracious as Anne believed?

2. How did the experience of the burglary on the night of April 11, 1944 affect Anne's sense of her own Jewish identity and the role of Jews in the world after the war?

Writing Activities:

1. Anne confided her feelings about Peter in her diary. Imagine you are Peter and write a diary entry describing your feelings for Anne. Or imagine that you are Anne's older sister Margot and comment upon the relationship you have seen growing between Anne and Peter.

2. Write about a time when you felt your parents or other adults in your life were being overprotective. Describe the issue over which you felt conflicted and tell whether it was resolved.

ANNE FRANK: THE DIARY OF A YOUNG GIRL

MAY 3, 1944 – AUGUST 1, 1944

Vocabulary: Analogies are word equations in which the first pair of words has the same relationship as the second pair of words. For example: DAY is to NIGHT as COMIC is to TRAGIC. Both pairs of words are opposites. Choose the best word from the Word Box to complete each of the analogies.

```
            WORD BOX
boisterous    prophecy      vain
liberation    supercilious
```

1. RECOLLECTION is to PAST as _____ is to FUTURE.

2. CALM is to MEDITATION as _____ is to RECREATION.

3. FREEDOM is to _____ as SADNESS is to DESPAIR.

4. HUMBLE is to _____ as WEALTHY is to IMPOVERISHED.

5. STARVED is to FAMISHED as ARROGANT is to _____.

Questions:

1. Why did Anne feel she could determine her own behavior toward Peter? Do you think she had a right to do so?

2. Why did Anne feel guilty about the letter she wrote to her father?

3. What event was everyone in the Annexe anxiously awaiting?

4. Why did the residents of the Annexe have to eat less?

5. Why was Anne disappointed in Peter?

6. How did D-Day affect the residents of the Annexe?

Questions for Discussion:

1. Commenting on the growing dislike for Jews, Anne quoted an old saying, "What one Christian does is his own responsibility, what one Jew does is thrown back at all Jews." What does this statement mean? In what ways is this statement true today?

2. Even with all the unhappiness and human frailties Anne had seen, she wrote, "I still believe that people are really good at heart." What did this reveal about Anne's character?

ANNE FRANK: THE DIARY OF A YOUNG GIRL

May 3, 1944 – August 1, 1944 (cont.)

Literary Device: Irony

Irony refers to an event that turns out to be the opposite of what is expected. As an observer of people, Anne was able to sense when a situation appeared ironic. Reread Anne's description of her parents' upbringing (May 8, 1944) and then the reaction of Anne and her family as Miep told them about an engagement party she had attended. Why did Anne find her family's reaction to Miep's story ironic?

_____
_____
_____

The epilogue tells you that the residents of the Secret Annexe were finally captured and sent to concentration camps. Why is this ending particularly ironic and heartbreaking?

_____
_____
_____
_____

Social Studies Connection:

Go to the library or search the Internet to find facsimile editions of newspapers printed on D-Day (June 6, 1944) and for two weeks that followed. Read about the landing as a military strategy and the difficulties faced by the allied army once it landed.

Writing Activity:

Imagine that Anne or Peter had survived their years in the Annexe and had been able to continue on with their lives. Write a diary entry that one of them might have written in March 1946, one year after the liberation of Holland.

LEARNING LINKS

CLOZE ACTIVITY

The following passage has been taken from the diary entry of April 4, 1944, in which Anne talks about her love of writing and her desire to become a journalist. Read the entire passage, and then go back to the beginning to fill in each blank with a word that makes sense in context. Afterward, you may compare your language with that of the author.

I am the best and sharpest critic of my own work. I know myself what is and _____(1)_____ is not well written. Anyone who doesn't _____(2)_____ doesn't know how wonderful it is; I _____(3)_____ to bemoan the fact that I couldn't _____(4)_____ at all, but now I am more _____(5)_____ happy that I can at least write. _____(6)_____ if I haven't any talent for writing _____(7)_____ or newspaper articles, well, then I can _____(8)_____ write for myself.

I want to get _____(9)_____; I can't imagine that I would have _____(10)_____ lead the same sort of life as Mummy _____(11)_____ Mrs. Van Daan and all the women who do _____(12)_____ work and are then forgotten. I must _____(13)_____ something besides a husband and children, something _____(14)_____ I can devote myself to!

I want _____(15)_____ go on living even after my death! _____(16)_____ therefore I am grateful to God for _____(17)_____ me this gift, this possibility of developing _____(18)_____ and of writing, of expressing all that _____(19)_____ in me.

I can shake off everything _____(20)_____ I write; my sorrows disappear, my courage _____(21)_____ reborn. But, and that is the great _____(22)_____, will I ever be able to write _____(23)_____ great, will I ever become a journalist _____(24)_____ a writer? I hope so, oh, I hope so very much, for I can recapture everything when I write, my thoughts, my ideals and my fantasies.

POST-READING ACTIVITIES

1. Return to the Anticipation Guide that you began in the Pre-Reading Activities on page four of this study guide. Fill in the "Anne" column. Compare your responses with those of your classmates.

2. Read the Afterward at the end of the book to get a better historical perspective on Anne's life and death. How did reading the Afterward affect your feelings about Anne and the people you read about in the *Diary*?

3. After reading *Anne Frank: The Diary of a Young Girl*, and the Supplement, how would you respond to those people who claim that the Holocaust never occurred?

4. What do you think has been the most important effect of publishing Anne Frank's diary? Do you think Anne might have made a greater impact on the world had she lived?

5. Read the copyright information at the beginning of the book. Notice that the diary has been published in many countries. Also notice that the original copyright was obtained by Otto H. Frank, Anne's father. If you had been in Otto Frank's place, would you have wanted your daughter's diary published?

6. Anne's diary is one of many memorials to Holocaust victims around the world. Do some research to find out the location of other living testimony to the Holocaust. If possible, visit the National Holocaust Museum in Washington, D.C.

7. **Cooperative Learning Activity:** Work with a small cooperative learning group to discuss the issue of whether the Holocaust could ever happen again. Try to reach a consensus of opinion within your group by giving each person the opportunity to present an opinion with strong arguments to support it. Compare your group's conclusion with those of other groups in your class.

8. Despite the fact that the Frank family was finally captured, the *Diary* can still be considered a story of survival. What human characteristics allowed these people to survive for as long as they did living in such difficult surroundings?

SUGGESTIONS FOR FURTHER READING

    Amothy, Christine. *I am Fifteen and I Don't Want to Die*. Scholastic.

    Appelman-Jurman, Alicia. *Alicia: My Story*. Bantam.

    Frank, Anne. *Anne Frank's Tales from the Secret Annex*. Bantam.

    Gies, Miep. *Anne Frank Remembered*. Simon & Schuster.

    Goldenberg, Linda. *In Kindling Flame, The Story of Hannah Senesh*. Valentine Mitchell.

* Greene, Bette. *Summer of My German Soldier*. Puffin.

* Hautzig, Esther. *The Endless Steppe*. HarperCollins.

    Hurwitz, Johanna. *Anne Franke: Life in Hiding*. HarperCollins.

* Kerr, M.E. *Gentlehands*. HarperCollins.

    Kuper, Jack. *Child of the Holocaust*. BerkleyTrade.

* Levitin, Sonia. *Journey to America*. Aladdin.

* Levoy, Myron. *Alan and Naomi*. Backinprint.com.

* Lowry, Lois. *Number the Stars*. Sandpiper.

* Matas, Carol. *Daniel's Story*. Scholastic.

    Mazer, Harry. *The Last Mission*. Laurel Leaf.

* McSwigan, Marie. *Snow Treasure*. Puffin.

* Reiss, Johanna. *The Upstairs Room*. HarperCollins.

    Richter, Hans P. *Friedrich*. Puffin.

    Siegal, Aranka. *Upon the Head of the Goat*. Square Fish.

    Suhl, Yuri. *They Fought Back*. Schocken.

    Wander, Fred and Hofmann, Michael. *Seventh Well*. Norton.

    Wiesel, Elie. *Dawn*. Hill and Wang.

* _____. *Night*. Hill and Wang.

* Yolen, Jane. *The Devil's Arithmetic*. Puffin.

* NOVEL-TIES Study Guides are available for these titles.

ANNE FRANK: THE DIARY OF A YOUNG GIRL

ANSWER KEY

June 14, 1942 – December 22, 1942
Vocabulary: 1. d   2. f   3. a   4. c   5. g   6. e   7. b   8. h;   1. trivial   2. devour   3. somber   4. fanatic   5. melancholy   6. obstinate   7. superfluous   8. optimism
Questions: 1. Anne decided to keep a diary after she received one as a birthday present. Because she wanted the diary to take the place of a close friend and confidante, she personalized it by calling it by a girl's name. 2. During the German occupation, the Frank family began to be affected by Hitler's anti-Jewish laws. Among other restrictions, they had to wear yellow stars, could not go to theaters, or take part in public sports. The girls went to special schools. Mr. Frank was no longer active in his own business. 3. These remarks related to the time when Anne and her family abandoned their home and went into hiding: life would never be the same again. 4. Dutch friends, such as Miep and Mr. Koophuis, helped the Franks go into hiding. 5. The Franks and the Van Daans hid in a few secret rooms in the warehouse of the company where Mr. Frank worked. 6. The family tried to stay busy, establishing routines whenever possible. The women cooked and prepared meals. Mr. Frank gave Anne lessons to continue her education. Books filled a lot of everyone's time. The warehouse rooms were "decorated" to make them as comfortable and familiar as possible. 7. On October 9, 1942 Anne recorded news about Jews being sent to death camps and the rumor that they were being gassed. 8. Anne felt fortunate that she was safely hiding, and she didn't want to live in gloom and despair.

January 13, 1943 – July 26, 1943
Vocabulary: 1. f   2. c   3. h   4. d   5. a   6. e   7. b   8. g;   1. cunning   2. aggressive   3. ceased   4. clandestine   5. rebukes   6. morale   7. wretched   8. indignant
Questions: 1. Anne believed she was fortunate because she felt that she was safe from being captured. The family also had money saved and food stored which allowed them to stave off hunger. She heard news about what was happening to other Jewish people and felt lucky by comparison. 2. During the war, everyone in Holland was suffering from a shortage of food, heat, and clothing. 3. Anne truly believed that her mother didn't show love to her, and now Anne was simply reflecting back this same indifferent attitude. Answers to the second part of the question will vary. 4. Anne felt like the favorite child because she was given a special poem from her father, and everyone gave her special things to celebrate her birthday. 5. Anne was becoming near-sighted and needed glasses. The family decided not to let Anne go out with Miep because this might put the entire family at risk. Also, because Anne had outgrown her clothes, strangers might become curious. 6. Conflict arose when Anne wanted to use the room twice a week in the afternoons to study. Dussel refused to allow this. Answers to the second part of the question will vary, but should include the idea that it would always be difficult for a staid, older man to share living quarters with a willful, thirteen-year-old girl. 7. Although the air raids signified British involvement in the war, they were dangerous and could have destroyed the Annexe.

July 29, 1943 – December 29, 1943
Vocabulary: 1. d   2. e   3. a   4. g   5. f   6. c   7. b;   1. tumult   2. pedantic   3. capitulate   4. inquisitive   5. exaggerate   6. hearty   7. tolerant
Questions: 1. The way the residents were forced to live placed them in highly unusual circumstances: they had to be extremely careful so that they wouldn't give themselves away. 2. The residents of the Annexe had to be as inert as possible during the day until the warehouse employees went home at 5:30. They feared that an unsympathetic worker could report them. 3. It was clear that Anne was depressed because she was taking Valerian pills, an anti-depressant, and admitted that she rarely laughed. 4. Elli had to help out more than usual because the others were sick and couldn't help. 5. Anne imagined Lies dressed in rags asking her for help. 6. Anne thought loneliness could be overcome if she were special to someone, his "one and only."

January 2, 1944 – March 12, 1944
Vocabulary: 1. A building complex consists of buildings that are joined together in some way. 2. If you have a mania for something, you have an unreasonably strong desire for it. 3. The expression that "something dawns on you" means that you discover something or that something becomes clear to you for the first time. 4. When you scrap a project, you give it up and decide not to complete it. 5. The embryonic stage of a project is its beginning.
Questions: 1. Anne sought out Peter Van Daan because she was lonely and wanted companionship. Answers

LEARNING LINKS

ANNE FRANK: THE DIARY OF A YOUNG GIRL

to the second part of the question will vary, but should include the ideas that both Anne and Peter were experiencing a sexual awakening and that their personalities complemented one another. 2. The people in the Annexe learned about the outside world from radio broadcasts, newspapers, and information brought to them by Koophuis, Henk, Miep, and Elli. The residents were most interested in the progress of the war and the work of the Underground Movement. 3. If Dutch citizens were caught helping Jews, they would be sent to concentration camps. 4. As they awaited the English invasion, the residents of the Annexe discussed whether or not it would be better to stay or leave the city. They made sure they had sufficient food and firewood because other people might want to stay with them. 5. While living in the Annexe, Anne believed that she had matured in many ways. The Anne who first went into hiding was amusing and superficial. She had become much more serious. She was better able to understand and tolerate the shortcomings of others, as well as her own. 6. Anne's mother believed thinking about the misery of others would help cure depression. Anne disagreed thinking enjoyment of nature was a better way to relieve sadness. Answers to the second part of the question will vary.

March 14, 1944 – May 2, 1944
Vocabulary: 1. adroit–skillful 2. hospitable–kind and accommodating 3. speculate–guess 4. discord–disagreement 5. sabotage–undermine 6. consolation– comfort
Questions: 1. Anne's internal conflict had to do with her growing affection for Peter and whether to act out of desire or to exercise common sense. 2. Anne needed "Kitty" as a place to confide her growing feelings for Peter. 3. Anne's cheerfulness and laughter helped Peter cope with life in the Annexe. 4. There were terrible shortages, many burglaries occurred because law had broken down, and children were ill and underfed. As difficulties for the citizenry increased, however, so did sabotage against the Germans in authority. 5. Anne dreamed that she would not become an ordinary housewife: she wanted to be a writer, perhaps a journalist. Answers to the second part of the question will vary. 6. The residents of the Annexe were afraid they would be discovered either by the burglars or by the police investigating the burglary. 7. April 15, 1944 was important to Anne because she received her first kiss from Peter. 8. Anne's father wanted Anne to be cautious in her relationship with Peter: he told her it was her responsibility to hold back. Answers to the second part of the question will vary.

May 3, 1944 – August 1, 1944
Vocabulary: 1. prophecy 2. boisterous 3. liberation 4. vain 5. supercilious
Questions: 1. Anne felt that the difficulty of life's circumstances made her mature and independent. As such, she had gained the right to make her own personal choices. Answers to the second part of the question will vary. 2. Anne felt guilty about the letter stating her independence because it hurt her father's feelings, making Anne feel as though she had been insensitive, overstating her case. 3. Everyone in the Annexe eagerly awaited the British invasion. 4. More and more people who were in hiding and helping those in hiding were being punished. Those who brought food to the Annexe were in great danger and had to reduce their activity. Thus, there was less food for those in the Annexe. 5. Anne was critical of Peter for still keeping his innermost thoughts to himself. She was disappointed in his distaste for religion and all his talk about food. He didn't seem mature, nor did he know what he wanted to do with his life. 6. After D-Day there was optimism in the Annexe because they saw an end to the war approaching. As the Germans were facing defeat, however, life in the occupied countries became more difficult. Food was scarce, money had no value, and more Jews were being sent to concentration camps.

NOTES: